T0091036

Behindfulness

for Beginners

A Parody Guide to Letting Sh*t Go,
Finding Inner Peace, and Staying Present

Dr. Harry B. Hind

ULYSSES
PRESS

Published in the US by:
ULYSSES PRESS
PO Box 3440
Berkeley, CA 94703
www.ulyssespress.com

ISBN: 978-1-64604-086-5
Library of Congress Control Number: 2021931500

Printed in the United States by Versa Press
10 9 8 7 6 5 4 3 2 1

Writer: Berni Johnson
Acquisitions editor: Keith Riegert
Managing editor: Claire Chun
Editor: Kathy Kaiser
Proofreader: Barbara Schultz
Cover design: Fiverr
Interior design: what!design @ whatweb.com
Layout: Jake Flaherty
Interior artwork: shutterstock.com

Contents

CHAPTER 1

Tame Your Animal Mind

And Then There Was Poop

Single-celled organisms and bacteria have been around for billions of years, but around 500 million years ago, more complex animal groups appeared—including the ancestors of all existing animals today. The first multicellular organisms (the first to eat and poop), appeared around 40 million years earlier. Australian biochemist Graham Logan hypothesizes that poop-producing animals set the stage for a boom in evolution.

Before them, plankton would photosynthesize and produce oxygen. When they died, bacteria would eat their remains and use up the oxygen, keeping the oceans high in carbon and low in oxygen. These new pooping animals ate the live plankton before the bacteria could do so, reducing the bacterial population. The poop (which carried off much of the carbon) would drop to the ocean floor, and more oxygen was released into the ocean water, paving the way for the evolution of multicellular creatures, which eventually led to you.

There are alternative theories about evolution, and we may never know the truth—but it's nice to hear good things about poop.

FIVE MINUTES IN THE HISTORY OF THE WORLD

Take five minutes to reflect on a recent start to a new track of your life.

_____

_____

_____

_____

_____

_____

_____

_____

_____

_____

Dino's for Dinner

Bits of fossilized feces are known as coprolites, and paleoscatologists and other researchers study them to find out what ancient animals ate. More coprolites of carnivorous dinosaurs exist today than those of herbivores because the minerals found in the bones of the prey of the meat eaters make the poop more likely to become fossilized. But there are still some herbivore coprolites out there.

Studying fossilized feces is one way we learn about dinosaur behavior. It shows us what they ate and tells us about their digestive systems. Herbivores have a separate chamber that we omnivores and carnivores don't have, which is full of bacteria that ferment the plant materials. Researchers are investigating the coprolites of these herbivores for indicators of methane levels, in an effort to shed light on climate change. So in a way, poop of the past may help us better understand our climate today.

Although we should all eat more fruits and veggies, we should avoid walking down the other paths of the herbivores. It isn't healthy to let things eat at you.

STOP LETTING THINGS EAT AT YOU

Fill these stinkers with all the individual things that are bothering you right now:

The Buzz on the Microbiome

Bees are herbivores who feed on plant nectar and pollen, and then spread this pollen from plant to plant, helping plants reproduce.

But these herbivores likely had a carnivorous waspy forebear. Bee species diversified over time, and today there are around 25,000 bee species. Flowering plants, which attract bees, evolved along with them.

 This change from carnivore to herbivore was partly enabled by gut flora, which let bees evolve into vegetarians. Corbiculate bee species (those that carry pollen in baskets on their hind legs) include honeybees, bumblebees, orchid bees, and stingless bees. Their microbiomes house bacteria that break down the sugars in pollen, nectar, and honey. So the symbiosis between bees and flowering plants is facilitated by the symbiosis between the gut bacteria and their bee hosts.

Bees are useful for studying gut microbiome evolution because their gut flora are relatively simple. Look at the creatures and you will learn about yourself, which points to the connection between everything in our ecosystem.

EVOLVE TOGETHER

Complete the first journal prompt during your bathroom session. Leave the second prompt for your partner to complete while in the bathroom.

Here are three things I'm grateful for:

1. _____

2. _____

3. _____

And here are three things I'm grateful for:

1. _____

2. _____

3. _____

Show Your Love

You can't live without pooping. But the dung beetle can't live without poop. There are three types of dung beetle: rollers, who roll dung into balls and bury them; dwellers, who live atop dung piles; and tunnelers, who burrow through dung into the ground underneath. Most dung beetles get their nutrients from herbivore dung.

During courtship, the male roller fashions a ball of dung and offers it to a female. If she accepts it, she either rides on top of the ball or helps roll it to a place where they bury it. After they mate, the female makes more balls of dung and lays an egg in each one. The larvae feed on the dung.

Dwellers lay their eggs in dung heaps, and tunneler females decorate their tunnels with dung in which they lay eggs. Tunnelers win the best parenting award because either one or both of the pair watch over the larvae.

Dung beetles fertilize the soil by loosening it and burying manure in it. And the ancient Egyptians believed that these insects keep the world turning.

WHAT MAKES YOUR WORLD TURN?

List five things you can't live without:

1. _____

_____

2. _____

_____

3. _____

_____

4. _____

_____

5. _____

The Art of Painted Turtle Breath

This practice comes to us from the North American eastern painted turtle, a creature that spends its fifty-plus years in the wild either basking in the sun when it's warm or hibernating underwater when it's cold. During its winter rest, it doesn't bother breathing—except through its skin and hindquarters. When its environment gets icy, the painted turtle lowers its temperature and metabolism, decreasing its need for oxygen.

But it still needs some oxygen. Instead of surfacing and taking a breath (a difficult feat when the lake is iced over), this resourceful reptile practices cloacal respiration, extracting oxygen from the water via its cloaca. The cloaca is an orifice found in reptiles, amphibians, birds, some fish, and a few mammals that serves multiple purposes, including all things reproductive and the excretion of urine and feces. Humans have a cloaca during embryonic development, but it divides into the bladder, rectum, and genitalia.

The butt breather's life is a simpler one, one of the purest calm. And one we should, at least in some respects, emulate.

BUTT-BREATHING EXERCISE

While sitting on the toilet, allow your butt cheeks to spread naturally.

Now close your eyes and cease breathing through your mouth; focus your attention on capturing the oxygen that becomes trapped in the bowl.

In your mind, repeat this mantra:

I am a hibernating turtle. I am at peace.
I no longer need my mouth to breathe.

After several minutes, if you haven't passed out, let your mouth breathing return, slowly. You are at peace. You should have an impression of gently running water passing effortlessly over the colorful shell of the universe.

Practice the Stillness
of the Wood Frog

The hibernation routine of wood frogs is even more peaceful than that of painted turtles. They simply settle in among the leaves on the ground and freeze solid, their heartbeats and respiration ceasing entirely. These little frogs remain in this state until they thaw, revive, and hop off on their merry way. They possess a natural antifreeze that keeps ice crystals from forming in their cells. Their urea levels go up during hibernation to around fifty times their normal non-hibernation amount, but their gut microbiome converts the urea into nitrogen, which also helps to protect them from the ill effects of the cold.

The human microbiome does many things for us, but this is not one of them. We will die if exposed to below-freezing temperatures long enough. So perhaps practice the stillness of the wood frog in the comfort of your heated home.

ONE MINUTE OF TOTAL FROG STILLNESS

Practice one minute of perfect stillness while sitting on the john. Seat yourself in a comfortable position, still your every limb, take a deep breath, and hold it for a few seconds to commune with the hibernating wood frog. Just make sure your heart keeps pumping.

CHAPTER 2

Letting Go of the Putrid Past

Banish Blame

The Peloponnesian War between Sparta and Athens broke out in 431 BCE. A year later, a plague struck Athens, killing one quarter to one third of the population over four years. Thucydides, a general and historian who got the plague and survived, described the symptoms: burning red eyes, red throat and tongue, terrible breath, sneezing, hoarseness, violent cough, vomiting, convulsions, blisters and sores, sleeplessness, diarrhea, amnesia, loss of eyesight, loss of fingers or toes, loss of genitals (likely to gangrene), and intense heat, which made some jump into wells for relief (and may have helped spread the disease through contaminated water).

There is still no consensus about the cause of the plague. Theories include measles, smallpox, ergotism (a fungal poison), a flu and staph infection combo, typhus, anthrax, or something humanity hasn't seen since.

Athenians accused Spartans of poisoning their reservoirs, but it is more likely that the disease spread through overcrowding and poor sanitation.

The lessons? Don't blame others for your misfortunes. And don't jump into communal wells.

COLOR AND LET GO

Slowly color in this cute puppy mandala. Would this puppy blame you for anything? No. So be like the puppy and let that shit go.

When in Rome, Don't Do as the Ancient Romans Did

We have learned much about ancient Rome from archaeological digs, including those at Pompeii, where a volcanic eruption in 79 CE entombed and preserved people going about their daily lives. The ancient Romans were a social lot, so social that they built public toilets without dividers, which could have kept them from fraternizing while they answered the call of nature. These toilets were long slabs of marble or other hard material with multiple holes at regular intervals (some were heated and some cold). Romans sat on these holes, and their waste dropped into flowing water that carried it away.

And the sharing didn't stop at toilet-side gossip. Romans at these communal commodes wiped with a tersorium, a sea sponge attached to a stick. They then rinsed the tersorium in a bucket of saltwater or vinegar, or perhaps under running water, and set it aside for use by the next person.

We can still learn from the Romans and work on our sense of community, because sharing is caring. Up to a point.

SHARING IS CARING

Make a list of five ways you would like to share with your community, be it cleaning up your local dog park, donating to a charity, or volunteering at a food bank. What will you give back? And don't say your used sponge.

1. _____

2. _____

3. _____

4. _____

5. _____

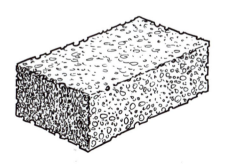

Urine for a Surprise

Poor ancient Romans didn't have access to fancy public toilets and had to collect and dispose of their own waste, likely in urns, unless the building they dwelled in had a foricae (a latrine shared by the residents).

There were also urns on roadsides and street corners, where the public could stop and pee. Some were placed there by fullers (launderers), who collected the urine and used it to clean and soften garments.

Emperor Vespasian had public urinals built so that he could sell the urine to fullers. Public urinals are still sometimes referred to as *vespasiani* in Italy.

Urine, human or animal, is rich in ammonia and was used by the ancient Romans to clean and whiten teeth!

Romans also used human urine, which is full of nitrogen and phosphorus, as a plant fertilizer, as part of the leather tanning process (urine to remove the hair and feces to soften the hide), and as a veterinary medicine (a use of dubious value). Kudos to the Romans for recycling, no matter how icky.

GARGLING FOR GRATITUDE

If you're like the rest of us, as soon as you start gargling mouthwash, you want to spit it out. Try this mindfulness exercise: Set a timer in your bathroom for one minute, and keep gargling while thinking of ten things you're grateful for. Repeat the list until your timer rings. We'll give you the first item:

1. I'm not gargling with urine. _____

2. _____

3. _____

4. _____

5. _____

6. _____

7. _____

8 _____

9. _____

10. _____

A Midsummer Night's Soil

In medieval Europe, people lived in walled towns, where they toiled for the castle-dwelling landowner. Roman plumbing had long since been destroyed by barbarian hordes. Many used chamber pots for their waste and either emptied them into outdoor holes (privy pits) or threw their contents out a window.

When the pits filled up, the excrement was shoveled out and carted off by *gongfermors*, or night-soil men (whose job persisted until the mid-nineteenth century, when sewers were built in large cities). The gongfermors might dump the waste on a dung heap outside the town wall or sell it as fertilizer. The residences of the wealthy might have privies with toilets that were merely a seat on top of a hole through which waste dropped into a chamber pot, barrel, pit, or flume (a channel for water). Or the waste might be thrown onto the ground outside or else into the castle moat.

There were notable exceptions: Christchurch Monastery at Canterbury (circa 1167), for example, had a complex sewer system with separate channels for running water, waste, and stormwater.

PRAISE THE PIPES

Say the following words of gratitude three times:

I am thankful for the porcelain that holds.

I am thankful for the bowl that catches.

I am thankful for the water that flushes.

I am thankful for the pipes that lead far, far away.

The Malodorous Middle Ages

In medieval Europe, people with money could bathe regularly, and some people still used public baths, despite the Catholic Church's view of naked mingling. The Benedictine monks at Westminster Abbey reportedly bathed just four times a year.

Plague in the 1300s made people increasingly wary of public baths, as they believed that illness entered through open pores. Some thought dirt provided a level of protection. For the less-than-rich, full-body bathing became less common. Soap was more likely to be used for clothes (although these might be washed in urine).

Then there were the cesspits, dung heaps, and waste from livestock. The populace was never far from poop.

In lieu of daily bathing, people wore perfume. And many carried pomanders, which they held to their noses to mask bad smells. These were pieces of fruit with embedded cloves or small containers filled with fragrant herbs and spices.

People erroneously thought pomanders protected them from infection, but the germs begged to differ.

AROMATHERAPY. WHERE IT'S NEEDED MOST.

To improve your mood and mask those pesky bathroom smells, let's try aromatherapy! Fill the air with the scent of lavender for stress, cinnamon for focus, peppermint for energy, or clove-studded oranges to ward off the Black Death.

Swine Before Pearls

New York may be a thriving metropolis with a large working class and a shortage of roaming livestock today, but this wasn't always the case. In the early 1820s, around 20,000 pigs wandered Manhattan, and these droves of street pigs persisted past the mid-nineteenth century.

The hog hordes served a purpose by eating garbage and waste (including human waste). But they left messes of their own and caused traffic accidents and other problems. People (erroneously) blamed cholera outbreaks and other public health issues on the sows.

Although they were faithful garbage collectors, the hogs weren't owned or hired by the city. They belonged to New York's poor residents, kept to convert to either food or money. Pigs were relatively cheap to raise, and the dearth of farmland meant the city's poor had few options for self-sufficiency. But richer residents objected to sharing their streets with swine. Consequently, the pigs were banished to the outskirts of the city around 1860. Eventually, the government made keeping pigs in the city illegal and hired garbage collectors to deal with the trash.

DEAL WITH YOUR TRASH

You don't have pigs to help you get rid of what you don't need. It's up to you. So let's start in the bathroom. Take a look through your medicine cabinet, under the sink, and in the shower, and find three things that you no longer have use for. Either recycle them or chuck them out!

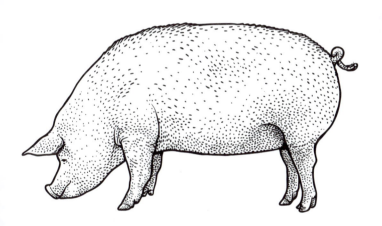

CHAPTER 3

Plumb the Depths

(Take) Waste Away

Sewers are not a modern invention, although most civilizations seemed to forget about them for many years, reviving their use in the latter half of the nineteenth century. Some of the first people known to have had complex wastewater systems were members of the Harappan civilization (aka the Indus Valley civilization) in what is now Pakistan and India, from around 3300 to 1700 BCE (perhaps longer in some areas).

Based on their ruins, we know that they were able to make uniformly sized, fire-baked, moisture-resistant bricks, and they used these bricks to build the first known urban sewer systems in their cities, to which even houses on the outskirts of the cities were connected. Inhabitants had wells from which to draw water, and wastewater was diverted into covered drains along the streets. The Harappans also built structures from these bricks that might have been public baths, but we may never know for sure. So far, no one has deciphered their written language.

CAPTURE YOUR OWN MOMENT IN TIME

Take five minutes to journal what your life is like right now.
Do this for future you and future generations.

_____

_____

_____

_____

_____

_____

_____

_____

_____

Let the Waters of Life Flow

We've all heard of the Roman aqueducts, but they were developed based on the water technologies of an earlier civilization, that of the Minoans of Crete. The Minoan civilization lasted from around 3200 to 1100 BCE. This ancient civilization built not only aqueducts of two types (open, gravity-driven aqueducts and closed, pressurized terra-cotta pipe aqueducts), but also rainfall collection systems, water filtration systems, cisterns, and fountains before anyone else is known to have done so.

They, or at least their palaces, also had indoor plumbing! Terra-cotta pipes and water taps supplied running water to these stately buildings, which also had some of the earliest indoor toilets (another contender is Neolithic Scotland, as we'll see on page 46).

Sadly, these relatively modern water and sewer technologies didn't catch on worldwide (or even Europe-wide), although as we'll see, the Romans tried their best. Perhaps the lesson is to appreciate our modern conveniences, especially the ones that provide us with water and take away our waste.

IMPROVE YOUR BATHROOM EXPERIENCE. TREAT YOURSELF.

Do as the Minoans did, and make your bathroom experience as pleasant and futuristic as possible. What are five gadgets you'd like to put on your bathroom's bucket list?

1. _____

2. _____

3. _____

4. _____

5. _____

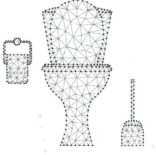

In Hot Water

The ancient Romans built aqueducts and sewers in Rome and across their conquered territories from around 312 BCE to 226 CE. Many of these advanced (for the time) water and sewage systems were later destroyed by barbarians or fell into disrepair, but parts of these systems still exist, with some in use today. The Trevi Fountain in Rome continues to be supplied by the Aqua Virgo aqueduct, which was built in 19 BCE.

The Romans were the first to use lead pipes. In fact, the word "plumbing" comes from *plumbus*, the Latin word meaning "lead." (The chemical symbol for lead, Pb, also derives from *plumbus*.) Cold and even hot running water were supplied via pipes and furnaces. The Romans built large public bathhouses with hypocausts (hollow areas) underneath the floor, which were filled with hot air from furnaces to warm the water. Sometimes they also exploited natural resources. The marble baths in Aquae Sulis, which is now the aptly named town of Bath in England, were built by the Romans over naturally occurring hot springs.

HAVE A DATE WITH YOUR PLUMBUS

Schedule a date to draw a hot bath.

Luxuriate in the cleansing water.

Relax.

(Feel free to invite a few friends in for a true Roman bathing experience.)

Embrace Your Spiritual Side

The ancient Romans had gods for nearly everything. Don't believe me? Meet Sterculius, the Roman god of dung. Roman farmers no doubt relied on him to provide fertilizer for the crops.

If you want to say a prayer to a goddess more adjacent to human waste expulsion, look to Venus Cloacina, the Roman goddess of sewers. She controlled the Cloaca Maxima (the Great Drain), where the drainage lines in Rome met and carried the city's wastewater to the Tiber River. A shrine was built to her in the Roman Forum, and her image appeared on Roman coins.

Fortuna, the Roman goddess of fortune, also played a role in citizens' daily excretions. Roman latrines were smelly and sometimes dangerous places, where you might be bitten by a rat or singed by a random hydrogen sulfide or methane explosion below. It was also believed that demons could emerge from the holes. Facilities had inscriptions to or statues of Fortuna for luck. We are indeed blessed that our modern bathrooms are mostly free of rats or fires or demons.

PAY YOUR RESPECTS

Create your own bathroom spirituality ritual.

Strike a match, light a candle, or burn some incense. Say a prayer, and if you don't have a chicken to sacrifice, pour a dash of mouthwash down the drain as an offering to the sewer goddess.

Out with the Bad Air, In with the Good

From the Middle Ages through the Victorian era, people thought that smelly vapors called miasmas caused disease. In London people did occasionally asphyxiate from gases (likely from old, covered-up cesspits) that got trapped in their homes when they sealed their windows against what they thought was the bad night air. But they were wrong about the source of illness. In the nineteenth and twentieth centuries, more and more was learned about the actual culprits—germs. It was also slowly discovered that many are spread by excrement.

So flushing your waste is a good thing. But flushing is not foolproof. Not washing your hands well (or at all) after using the bathroom can spread fecal bacteria. And flushing the toilet can aerosolize particles of feces and throw them into the air. These particles can hang in the air for hours and land on anything within a few feet of your toilet. If you want inner peace, don't think about them landing on your toothbrush. And flush with the lid down.

ENJOY THE FRESH AIR

Because we don't have to worry about miasmas anymore, try this highly effective 4-7-8-4 breathing exercise to relieve stress and anxiety the next time you're taking a squat.

1. With your mouth closed, inhale through your nose to the count of 4.

2. Close your eyes and hold your breath to the count of 7.

3. Open your eyes and audibly (*whoosh*), slowly exhale through your mouth to the count of 8.

Repeat until you've completed four breath cycles.

Spread Love, Not Germs

Although we have evolved beyond flinging our excrement at each other, poop still afflicts us. Dysentery, cholera, and typhoid are three poop-borne diseases. You can get them from feces-contaminated water, from insects that land on poop, or, in the case of typhoid, via close contact with the infected or with people who neglect handwashing.

Filth-aided outbreaks were common until the mid-nineteenth century, when cities modernized their sewer systems and instituted street cleaning and garbage pickup. Queen Victoria's husband, Prince Albert, died in 1861, likely of typhoid.

Sometimes people are vectors of infection. Mary Mallon (Typhoid Mary) was a cook in New York at the turn of the twentieth century. An asymptomatic carrier of typhoid, she spread the disease to at least 122 people. She was quarantined twice, the second time for twenty-four years, until her death.

Waste-borne illnesses still occur today. Here in the United States, food is periodically recalled due to contamination with E. coli from animal waste. Romaine, anyone?

A MOMENT OF MINDFUL COLORING

Clear your mind while coloring in these adorable bacteria.

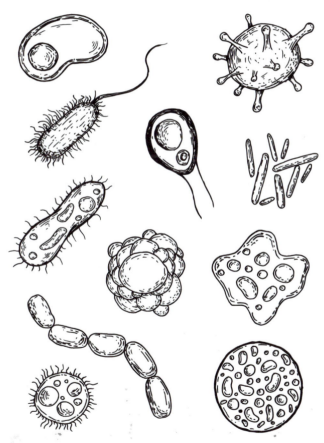

The Great Stinks

It was once customary for waste to be diverted directly into waterways. In the nineteenth century it was discovered that human waste causes disease, and cities began improving their sewer systems.

In London Joseph Bazalgette oversaw construction of a new sewage system. The impetus for the project was likely the 1858 "Great Stink of London," an overwhelming odor emanating from the Thames, which caused the meeting of Parliament nearby to be suspended. Most of the city was connected to the new sewer system by 1866. It diverted the wastewater to treatment facilities farther downriver.

In 1852 Eugène Belgrand started building a new sewer system in Paris. The construction, completed in the 1860s, was so attractive that people went on guided tours of the sewer. Boats pushed the waste into the river Seine. Regrettably, the river was too slow-moving to drive the waste toward the ocean, and the waste lingered near the banks. Consequently, Paris had two great stinks, one in 1880 and another in 1895.

The moral? Don't make a stink about annoyances but rather choose peace.

APPRECIATE THE THINGS THAT SMELL GOOD

List five smells that make you feel happy.

1. _____

_____

2. _____

_____

3. _____

_____

4. _____

_____

5. _____

_____

CHAPTER 4

Live in the Moment

Flush Away Your Worries

Two civilizations contend for recognition as the inventor of indoor flush toilets: the Minoan civilization of Crete (detailed on page 32) and Neolithic Scotland around 3000 BCE, although the Scots likely flushed manually with bins of water.

The flush toilet was reinvented in 1592 by Sir John Harington. He built two, one for Queen Elizabeth I at Richmond Palace and one for himself. A cistern of water above the toilet was attached to a pipe to flush away waste. Unfortunately, no more were built.

In 1775 watchmaker Alexander Cummings patented a "valve closet" design with an S-trap (the curved pipe at the bottom of the toilet) that flushed with a swirl of water in the bowl. In 1778 Joseph Bramah improved on Cummings' design and sold thousands of expensive toilets.

In 1861 Prince Edward of England hired Thomas Crapper to build lavatories with flushing toilets in the royal palaces. Others also produced toilets during this time. Thank these inventors for enabling us to flush away our excreta and live pleasant-smelling, cholera-free lives.

LEARN HOW TO FLUSH

We are indeed fortunate to have modern indoor plumbing. But do you truly appreciate it? Do you even know how your toilet works? Try taking this short quiz by matching up the numbers with the parts of your commode.

_____Outlet   _____Bowl   _____Weir

_____Tank   _____Ballcock   _____Inlet

_____Flapper   _____Float Ball   _____Water Seal

                                     _____Trapway

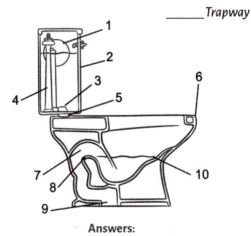

Answers:

9. Outlet; 2. Tank; 3. Flapper; 6. Bowl; 4. Ballcock; 1. Float Ball; 8. Weir; 5. Inlet; 10. Water Seal; 7. Trapway

47

Tea for Number Two

Thomas Twyford, a contemporary of Thomas Crapper, began his career as a pottery maker, including teapots. In 1849 he also began making chamber pots. Upon his death, his son Thomas William Twyford took over the company. In 1883 he released a design called the Unitas, a fully exposed, single-piece ceramic toilet with a hinged seat. Cheaper and easier to clean than its predecessors, this toilet was shipped all over. *Unitas* even became the Russian word meaning "bathroom."

Another famous toilet maker was John Doulton. In 1815 he invested all his money in a pottery and pipe manufacturing company. John Doulton's son Henry followed his father into the company. He hired artists from the Lambeth School of Art, including many women. The company also produced tiles and other decorative items. Henry Doulton eventually received a knighthood, and the company was given permission to call itself Royal Doulton in 1901. It later became better known for its fine china.

Because pottery artisans produced toilets in the Victorian era, these ceramic wares were often ornately designed and beautifully colored. Tea, anyone?

TEE UP MORE IMPROVEMENT

The Twyford clan certainly improved your life. Let's pay it forward. What is one thing you can do to give a helping hand to someone in your life?

_____

_____

_____

_____

_____

_____

Treat Yourself—and Your Waste

Cities began installing sewage treatment facilities in the late nineteenth century. In the United States in the 1930s, about half of the homes had indoor plumbing. Now most are hooked up to sewers, although some still rely on septic tanks.

At a sewage treatment plant, wastewater is filtered and treated to remove or neutralize solid waste, biodegradable organic materials, chemical pollutants, and pathogens. The wastewater moves through screens, which filter out large solids, and through sedimentation tanks, where smaller solids settle to the bottom and are scraped away. In most developed nations, microbes are used to eat remaining organic materials. The water might be disinfected with chlorine or ultraviolet radiation.

The sludge might be treated with bacteria, chemicals, enzymes, or heat to destroy pathogens. Some treatment plants use methane produced by these processes to power themselves.

You may not appreciate the smell as you drive by your friendly neighborhood sewage treatment plant, but better there than the whole neighborhood.

NOW CLEAN UP YOUR ACT

What are five ways you could detoxify, reset, and rid your body or mind of bad habits? (Think of these bad habits as your sewage, which is currently being released into your favorite river, the River You.)

1. _____

2. _____

3. _____

4. _____

5. _____

Touch or No Touch

Hospitals must keep germs to a minimum to prevent spreading illness to already injured or unwell patients. Toward this end, some have installed automatic, hands-free faucets, which let water flow once the presence of hands is detected. It was thought that these faucets would both cut down on germs left by people's hands touching the handles and also save water.

Hospitals did save water. But it turned out that the water passing through these automatic taps was more likely to be contaminated with bacteria than the water in the manual predecessors. A 2011 Johns Hopkins study found that cultured water samples from 50 percent of automatic taps contained Legionella bacteria, compared with 15 percent of manually controlled taps. A 2020 study at the University of Bologna, Italy, likewise found a higher incidence of Legionella bacteria in automatic versus manual taps.

Some hospitals have switched back to manual faucets. The old way was a better way. But medical staff shouldn't go too far back, say to the not-so-good old days of doctors not washing their hands.

REVERT TO THE PAST

For the next week, try this challenge. Instead of bringing your phone into the can with you (gross), fill your time on the throne with some old-timey activities such as these:

- Read a poem.

- Browse a newspaper.

- Do a crossword puzzle.

- Crochet something adorable.

- Stare blankly at the wall.

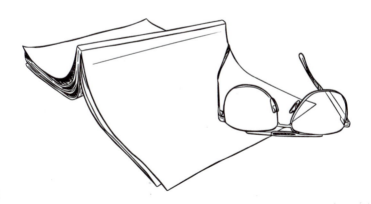

The Fatberg(s) of London

Sewer blockages are never pleasant, but imagine one that weighs 130 tons and is as solid as a rock. A fatberg of this description formed in 2017 in the sewers of London underneath Whitechapel. Fatbergs consist mainly of nonflushable (but flushed anyway) items, such as wet wipes or diapers, combined with cooking oils and fats that have been poured down the drain. As well as being huge, expensive nuisances, they are also regular occurrences. A 15-ton fatberg had to be cleared from around Kingston in 2013, and a 40-ton one was cleared from the sewer at Greenwich in 2019. It takes many wastewater workers several weeks to remove each one.

The silver lining of the 2017 fatberg is that it was sent to a processing plant and converted into biodiesel rather than buried in a landfill. Presumably, later ones were and will be, as well. But this is a highly inconvenient way to produce energy. Channel your inner sewage worker and throw your refuse (and cooking fats) in the trash can.

TRANSFORM THAT SH*T

You know you're holding onto your own fatberg of emotion. Well, now's your chance to convert that fatberg into emotional fuel. What's been bothering you recently?

_____

_____

_____

_____

_____

_____

_____

_____

_____

Mentioning the Unmentionable

Going to the bathroom is something we all do. It's a natural and necessary bodily function. But it's also a taboo subject in many cultures. We rarely speak of bathroom stuff, especially the actual process and its end products. The closer we get to actually describing what we're going to do, the more crass it's considered. Instead, we employ euphemisms for anything related to it, such as, "answer the call of nature," "powder my nose," or "see a man about a dog." In England you might "spend a penny," derived from the fact that public toilets once cost a penny to use.

Case in point: In New York City in 1789, the first US Congress was meeting. Nearby, a camel was on public display. When one of these early US political leaders had to go to the bathroom, he would say that he was going out to see the camel.

You needn't be ashamed of your daily bathroom journeys. But you can still have fun with the language if you want to.

POOP BREAK

Take a breather and color in this unmentionable word for a moment of mindful fun.

CHAPTER 5

Mind, Body, and Soul—But Mostly Body

The Journey's Beginning

Your digestive system is mostly a tube that runs from your mouth to your anus. This tube pushes your food along via peristalsis, whereby muscles in the gastrointestinal organs relax in front of food to allow it to pass and contract behind food to push it forward. But you start digesting the food you eat when you put it in your mouth and start chewing and swishing the food around with your teeth and tongue.

Chewing itself breaks down the food a little, and your saliva contains substances that dissolve particles so that your taste buds can sense the flavors. Bacteria in your mouth also start processing your food (but their counterparts in the large intestine do the bulk of bacterial digestion). Once you swallow, the food goes down your throat and into your stomach, where slower and more intense processes of digestion begin.

And when you cook food, digestion starts before you even put food in your mouth. Cooking is a form of pre-digestion, which makes it much easier for your gut to deal with the food you eat.

LET'S CLEAN THAT SYSTEM

Choose one of the following foods that are super high in intestine-scrubbing fiber, and make a promise to get it into your diet before the end of the next five days.

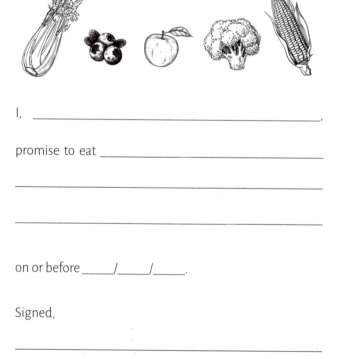

I, _____,

promise to eat _____

_____

_____

on or before _____/_____/_____.

Signed,

_____

Comfort-Giving Saliva

Two to four pints of saliva—consisting of water, mucus, mineral salts, proteins, and enzymes—are produced in the salivary glands in your mouth daily. Saliva kicks off the digestive process. Its main enzyme, salivary amylase, starts to break down carbohydrates into a sugar in your mouth.

The mucus in saliva helps coat boluses of chewed food so they slide down your throat easily. Saliva also contains antimicrobial substances.

Saliva makes dry foods more soluble, and keeps your mouth lubricated and comfortable. Dry mouth can be a symptom of disease, including diabetes, Parkinson's, Sjögren's syndrome, or HIV/AIDS. Or it can result from stress, smoking, chemotherapy, radiation therapy, or certain medications. Alternatively, it may indicate that you are dehydrated and need to drink some water.

Scientists recently discovered a new aspect of saliva. This secretion contains a pain-killing substance, opiorphin, that is more potent than morphine!

So drool away, and rejoice in the comforting presence of saliva.

MOUTH FEEL

Close your eyes and let your salivary glands do their work by sucking the multitasking substance called mucus out of your glands and swishing it around in your mouth. Note how this makes your mouth feel. If you are so inclined, hold your mouth open and breathe for a while until your mouth dries out.

What do you notice?

_____

_____

_____

_____

_____

_____

Cleansing and Healing Flow

The flow of saliva during waking hours keeps your mouth and teeth clean, helping to prevent gum disease and tooth decay. Minerals and proteins in your saliva also help strengthen your tooth enamel. Saliva increases when you chew or suck on food or candy, when you eat spicy or acidic food, when you brush your teeth, and sometimes when you just think about food. Saliva production slows during sleep, allowing bacteria to flourish and resulting in morning breath. All the more reason to brush your teeth before and after sleep.

Saliva can be a diagnostic tool. Testing saliva to detect hormones, proteins, and other tiny molecules to predict and diagnose health issues is becoming more common as sensors are being developed that can detect nano-scale molecules. No needles are involved. At-home saliva tests for thyroid hormone levels are already on the market. And you can get a DNA analysis by sending your saliva to a lab.

Take a moment to silently praise the flow of this cleansing, healing liquid.

THE MORNING BREATH OF LIFE

Everything in life is temporary, including morning breath. What are a few struggles in your life that are bound to pass with time (and maybe a little gum)?

_____

_____

_____

_____

_____

_____

_____

_____

_____

Tongue in Cheek

Your tongue helps you chew, swallow, suck on, and taste food and drink—and also speak.

The tongue is composed of muscle, connective tissue, and glands, and covered in a mucous membrane (the mucosa). Tongue muscles are arranged in three directions, allowing complex movements. The upper tongue is covered in two types of papillae (nodules). Mechanical papillae keep the mucous membrane attached to the tongue and sense the feel of food. Taste papillae contain taste buds. Each taste papilla has 50 to 150 taste receptor cells, and each receptor can detect one taste: bitter, salty, sour, sweet, or umami.

The tongue also has serous glands, which excrete the clear portion of saliva, and mucous glands, which secrete mucus. Instead of papillae, the rear of the tongue has lymphatic tissue called lingual tonsils, which help detect toxins and microbial invaders. They are part of the immune system's tonsillar ring, which also includes the tonsils and the adenoids.

The tongue connects to the hyoid bone and voice box.

Go ahead: wag your tongue and vocally appreciate its gifts.

INTRO TO TONGUE YOGA

Stick out your tongue. Move it up toward the sky, and hold this position for a few seconds. Then all the way to the right and hold. Then down toward the floor and hold. Then all the way to the left and hold. Then perform four clockwise circles and four counterclockwise circles. Then let your mouth companion rest. Namaste.

A Lump (of Food) in Your Throat

Like the tongue, the esophagus is composed of muscle lined with mucosa. About one inch wide and eight inches long, it resides in front of the spine and behind the heart and trachea, and goes through the diaphragm. Some of the muscle is arranged spirally to allow the elasticity necessary for peristalsis to push food down the throat.

The esophagus has two bundles of muscles that open and close: the upper esophageal sphincter and the lower esophageal sphincter. The upper keeps food and liquid from entering the windpipe, and opens up to allow food and drink to pass when you swallow. The lower is at the entrance to the stomach and prevents acid and other stomach products from traveling back up (except during vomiting, belching, or heartburn). This lower sphincter is attached at the right-hand side of the stomach, so that when abdominal muscles press on the bottom of the stomach during movement, food isn't pushed out the top.

Standing or sitting up helps the esophagus to narrow and close fully, which prevents heartburn after you eat.

KANTHAH STRETCH

Practice stretching your esophagus by sitting up straight on the toilet. Place your feet firmly on the floor in front of your throne, and your hands on your knees. Hold your head high, as though it were attached to the ceiling by a string. Straighten your neck and spine, and keep those gastric juices where they belong.

Learn to Stomach Your Digestive Processes

The next stop after the esophagus is the stomach, a crescent-shaped bag that holds food for a while and lets gastric acids and enzymes break down what you've chewed still further, eventually turning it to mush. Simple carbohydrates break down quickly, but proteins and fats can take hours, so how long food remains there varies. The right side of the stomach, where the lower esophageal sphincter empties into that organ, is shorter than the left side, accounting for the organ's lopsided shape.

Most of us, when placing our hands where we think is in front of the stomach, are actually aiming too low. The stomach starts around the left nipple and ends below the bottom of the right-hand ribs.

The stomach is lined with muscles called rugae, which contract and relax to further mix your food. Once your stomach is done with its contents, it opens the pyloric sphincter to allow the food to pass into the small intestine.

MIND THE STOMACH

Let's call this an exercise in patience. Sit still, put your hand on your belly—no, a little higher—and feel its rumblings. Praise be to the churning of your stomach.

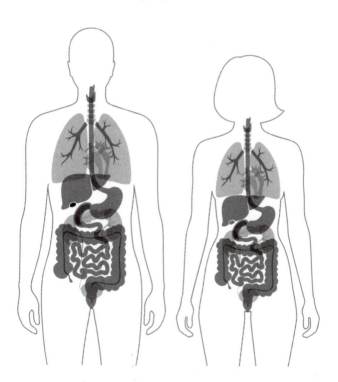

Journey Through the Twisty Intestines

Once the mush that was once our food reaches the small intestine, it begins a long and twisty journey. Coiled inside the gut, the small intestine is ten to twenty feet long. Its inner lining is covered in villi (tiny, fingerlike structures), giving it an enormous surface area. In the small intestine, food is broken down still further into molecules the body can use. Anything it can't break down gets passed via the ileocecal valve into the large intestine, where it continues on a much slower portion of the journey (perhaps sixteen hours).

The large intestine is a smooth tube about three feet long that surrounds the small intestine. During peristalsis, parts of it look lumpy. The large intestine houses most gut bacteria, which further break down the leftovers, dredging out more nutrients (such as calcium), feeding on what they need, and producing fatty acids and vitamins that *you* need. The large intestine also reclaims water from the mush. In the large intestine, the leftovers form a stool, which you'll expel through the rectum and out the anus.

FIND YOUR WAY THROUGH

Take a moment or two to try to solve this maze. This is what your food has to do every single day (hopefully).

Bypassing the Gut

Practicing slowness is calming, but sometimes things need to be fast-tracked. There are two parts of the digestive system where you can administer medications directly and bypass the stomach and intestines (as well as the liver, which metabolizes meds), sending meds straight into the bloodstream.

The first is the beginning of the digestive system, the smooth, papilla-free underside of your tongue. Some medications, such as nitroglycerin for angina, are placed or sprayed under the tongue (sublingually), where they are absorbed by the mucous membrane. They quickly enter the circulatory system and get to work.

The other is the anus, the last two or so inches of the digestive system. The anus will give anything in a suppository an express ticket into the circulatory system. For this reason, suppositories have lower doses of medicine than would be needed in a pill. With pills, you have to account for a lot of the active ingredients getting weeded out by the liver. Like sublingual meds, medications in suppository form take effect more quickly.

JUMP AHEAD

Come up with three shameless shortcuts that will make your tasks a little easier. You can't always take the slow path to enlightenment.

1. _____

_____

_____

2. _____

_____

_____

3. _____

_____

_____

What We Expel

Feces are produced in the large intestine. Most of the water used in digestion is reabsorbed here, but enough is left in the feces to make them easy to expel (in the absence of constipation). Feces are about three-fourths water (less when a person is constipated, more when a person has diarrhea). That last one quarter or so of solid material is around one-third indigestible fiber, one-third dead bacteria (mostly E. coli), and one-third stuff the body needs to get rid of, such as cholesterol, medicines, or food additives.

The more plant fiber you ingest, the larger your bowel movements, which can range from 3½ ounces to 18 ounces. BMs are usually brown, mostly due to blood corpuscles the body needs to expel. Blood corpuscles travel from the liver to the intestines, where gut bacteria turn them brown. Fecal discoloration (too light or too dark) can indicate illness or internal injury.

The Bristol stool chart categorizes feces from type 1 (dry, hard lumps) to type 7 (entirely liquid). Types 3 and 4 (sausage-shaped) are ideal.

NOTICE WHAT YOU LOST

Examine your poop and rate it via the Bristol stool chart.
How are things looking?

TYPE 1		Rabbit Droppings	Separate hard lumps
TYPE 2		Bunch of Grapes	Sausage-shaped, but lumpy
TYPE 3		Corn on the Cob	Like a sausage but with cracks on its surface
TYPE 4		Sausage	Like a sausage or snake, smooth and soft
TYPE 5		Chicken Nuggets	Soft blobs with clear cut edges
TYPE 6		Porridge	Fluffy pieces with ragged edges, a mushy stool
TYPE 7		Gravy	Watery, no solid pieces, entirely liquid

You. Are. Not. Alone.

In this frenetic modern age of social media, streaming content, and self-driving cars, it's easy to find yourself feeling detached from other living things. When you find yourself pitching toward loneliness, remember this incredibly comforting thought—you are not alone; in fact, you are never alone. You have 100 trillion bacteria living in your digestive tract. Bacteria make up something like 90 percent of all the cells in your body! Your cells do, however, outweigh them. The microbes account for about one to two kilos of your actual weight. That's a full pound or two of living, swimming friends who are along for this wild ride called your life.

Most of them, thankfully, are good bacteria, which provide you with myriad health benefits, including training your immune system, producing vitamins, helping with digestion, and detoxifying some substances. So maintain good nutrition to keep your little passengers thriving, and you need never feel lonely again.

RELEASE THAT DEAD BAGGAGE

Of course, not all the bacteria inhabiting your intestines are healthy for you. Some are quite literally toxic. And like other toxic things in your life, letting go is an absolute must. That's why 10 to 20 percent of what you poop every day are dead bacteria, which no longer belong in your life. It's your body's way of saying, *It's time for a change.*

**What other toxic things in your life
are you ready to expel?**

_____

_____

_____

_____

_____

_____

The Three Types of People

In 2011 researchers discovered that people belong in one of three categories, dubbed enterotypes, based on the dominant strain of bacteria in their microbiome: Bacteriodes, Prevotella, and Ruminococcus (although some doubt the validity of the last enterotype). Your category provides clues about how well you handle certain foods, whether you are prone to obesity or type 2 diabetes, and how you will react to various medical treatments.

These groups are found worldwide, with some regional differences. More than 50 percent of Japanese people have bacteria that result in soy reducing their risk of heart disease, prostate cancer, or bone disorders, but only 25 to 30 percent of people of European descent receive the same benefits from these bacteria.

Bacteriodes, more common in heavy meat eaters, produce enzymes that break down carbs to efficiently extract energy. Prevotella, more common in vegetarians, are good at finding proteins. Ruminococcus, which exist in the gut, produce heme, necessary for blood production. Whether they are truly a marker of a third group is debated.

WHERE DO YOU BELONG?

List the various groups you belong to (and take a guess as to your enterotype).

_____

_____

_____

_____

Now list a few groups you aspire to belong to.

_____

_____

_____

_____

_____

_____

Chewing Our Food for Us

Your gut bacteria digest some things you can't, providing you with the resulting energy. In fact, 10 percent of your nutrition is produced by your gut biome. But some microbial digestion and nutrient production start before you eat.

Bacteria are responsible for fermentation, which preserves food. It also provides health benefits, due in part to the good bacteria (probiotics) in fermented foods.

Yogurt is milk that bacteria have mostly digested for you by breaking down its lactose into lactic acid. Kefir is another fermented milk product. Miso is fermented soy, kombucha is fermented tea, and pickles are fermented cucumbers. Sauerkraut (fermented cabbage) has the bacteria lactobacillus plantarum, which boost the immune system and keep yeast in check. Bacteria can also produce vitamins, giving fermented foods additional nutrients.

Bacteria (and sometimes fungi) also make the production of cheeses, sausages, and sourdough bread possible. Thank them the next time you make a cheese on sourdough sandwich, and wash it down with kombucha.

STOP GNAWING ON THAT

You don't have to do everything on your own. Remind yourself that it is okay to accept help from others. Make a gratitude list of those who have helped you along the way.

_____

_____

_____

_____

_____

_____

_____

_____

_____

_____

Moderate Your Spirits

Alcoholic beverages are also fermented, but the bacteria don't survive production. Still, a glass of wine, beer, or other liquor can be enjoyable and conducive to good health. Much of the enjoyment is thanks to microbes, too. Not only are microorganisms (in this case, yeasts) used to produce alcohol, but some of the taste you experience is due to bacteria at the back of your tongue processing them and releasing substances that give off an aftertaste.

Unfortunately, drinking alcohol greatly increases the population of bacteria that produce gas. It can also make the gut temporarily more porous, resulting in short-lived food sensitivities, such as gluten intolerance, and can lead to reflux by weakening the esophageal sphincters. If too much alcohol is ingested all at once, the gut will inform the brain, sometimes triggering vomiting to rid the body of the influx of toxins.

One daily serving for women and two for men is the recommended limit. This sensible intake decreases the risk of kidney stones, heart disease, stroke, and even Alzheimer's disease. All things in moderation.

ONE TEQUILA, TWO TEQUILA, THREE TEQUILA...

What did you drink this week? How much? How did it make you feel (on a scale from mildly lubricated to unconscious)?

MONDAY	Sober	Mildly Lubricated	Unconscious
TUESDAY	Sober	Mildly Lubricated	Unconscious
WEDNESDAY	Sober	Mildly Lubricated	Unconscious
THURSDAY	Sober	Mildly Lubricated	Unconscious
FRIDAY	Sober	Mildly Lubricated	Unconscious
SATURDAY	Sober	Mildly Lubricated	Unconscious
SUNDAY	Sober	Mildly Lubricated	Unconscious

The Perils of Intolerance

Many people have trouble breaking down lactose (milk sugars). Lactose intolerance can cause nausea, vomiting, bloating, gas, and diarrhea. The lactose-intolerant person usually manufactures too little of the enzyme lactase in the small intestine, which is responsible for breaking down lactose, so much of the lactose remains intact and wanders into the large intestine, where bacteria begin to work away at it. This is where symptoms arise. The problem can be induced by illness, injury, or certain medications, and may be reversible when the underlying issue is dealt with. But it can also be congenital.

People with lactose intolerance can eliminate dairy from their diet, ingest specially processed low-lactose or no-lactose milk or other dairy products, or even take a lactase enzyme (available in drops or pills). Probiotics may also help prevent some symptoms. Those with lactose intolerance may be able to digest yogurt and kefir because much of the lactose digestion has already taken place. Hard cheeses also have less lactose than soft cheeses. So all is not lost for the intolerant dairy lover.

A DAILY AFFIRMATION

Repeat this affirmation at least once daily:

I am flushing away hate. Through patience and peace, I am growing stronger in tolerance and love.

Gut Deforestation

The microbiome is sometimes called the gut flora because scientists used to (erroneously) classify bacteria as part of the plant family. But a teeming forest is an apt metaphor for the gut ecosystem. You rely on the huge number of friendly bacteria in your digestive system (which reside mainly in the large intestine). But you might unwittingly do things to depopulate the "flora."

Not eating enough fiber or other nutrients is one way to adversely affect your microbiome. The bacteria that thrive on plant matter, for instance, can die off if you don't feed them fruits, vegetables, and grains.

Heavy antibiotic use can depopulate the microbiome because these medicines kill bacteria. Illnesses, especially those that lead to diarrhea, can also wash away much of your biome in one fell swoop.

And simply living in an urban setting also seems to have a detrimental effect. A study of the Hadza, a hunter-gatherer tribe in Tanzania, found that they had twice as much microbiome diversity as the average city dweller. A microbiome study of a tribe on the Amazon yielded similar results.

OPEN YOURSELF TO NATURE

In this minute of Zen, open the bathroom window and breathe in deeply, accepting nature. (If needed, leave that window open a crack. Your housemates will thank you.)

Color Me Surprised

A disease that turns urine red may have inspired the legend of vampires. Acute hepatic porphyria is a rare genetic defect that prevents the body from making heme (a component of red blood cells). More common in women than men, other symptoms include sensitivity to garlic and sunlight, rapid or irregular heartbeat, high blood pressure, seizures, abdominal pain or swelling, nausea, constipation, diarrhea, mood changes, hallucinations, fatigue, insomnia, numbness in the arms and feet, weakness in the belly, arms, or legs, and paralysis. Those with this disorder may also have low levels of sodium or magnesium in their blood. Treatment exists, but the illness is often misdiagnosed.

Other possible causes of reddish or pinkish urine are kidney stones or cysts, a urinary tract infection, an enlarged prostate, a tumor, certain medications, or eating beets, rhubarb, or blackberries.

There are also illnesses, medications, dyes, and foods that turn your urine orange, blue, green, brown, or cloudy. So pay attention to your pee. It may be trying to tell you something.

A RAINBOW OF URINE

Color in all the hues you can imagine hitting the bowl.

Your Not-So-Useless Friend

The appendix is a small, thin organ about four inches long and shaped somewhat like a finger. It rests near where the small and large intestines meet, usually in the lower right of the abdominal cavity. Many people think it's a useless organ, a leftover from an evolutionary stage. And we can indeed live without the appendix. It has a tendency to become inflamed or infected and even to rupture (a condition known as appendicitis), necessitating its removal. Once it's out, its absence doesn't seem to cause any obvious health problems.

But some researchers believe it's more useful than previously thought. They theorize that it acts as a storehouse for good bacteria. When you have diarrhea or take a round of antibiotics, many good bacteria are killed or flushed from your system. After this sort of catastrophe, some believe that the helpful little appendix repopulates your gut flora. So if it's still around, you should apologize to the unsung hero of your gut. After decades of disparagement, it can probably use a self-esteem boost.

APPEND A MOMENT OF GRATITUDE

If you still have your appendix, express your gratitude to this little-recognized paragon of the gut.

If you don't, observe a moment of silence on the john for your dearly departed organ—and take a probiotic just in case.

Digestive Discord

As soon as you swallow food or drink, a process called peristalsis begins to move it through your digestive tract. The esophagus pushes the food toward the stomach. After mixing with digestive fluid in the stomach, the matter is pushed into the small intestine, which breaks it down further for absorption by the body. Any matter that is not transferred to the bloodstream is pushed to the large intestine as waste, where some water reclamation occurs and where the waste is processed by your friendly neighborhood gut bacteria. The leftovers are transformed into stool. The large intestine moves the processed waste to your rectum, where it is eventually pushed out through the anus.

Peristalsis sometimes leads to a phenomenon called a borborygmus, which is a growling or rumbling sound in your gut. The natural passage of the solids and fluids through your digestive system can cause this sound, but gases trapped in your gut (including air you have swallowed and gases that are by-products of digestion, often produced by your gut bacteria) can cause louder, more embarrassing bouts of borborygmi, usually during quiet moments in crowded public places.

FINDING THAT INNER PIECE

The next time your gut rumbles or squeals, observe the noise and accept it without judgment. Be aware of sensations as you let the ingested food, drink, and trapped gases flow through you. Cast your mind upon the transformations they are undergoing on their long journey as the nutrients make their way into your body, and the leftover waste moves on to its final resting place. And if others happen to be within earshot, explaining the mechanics behind the phenomenon in detail is a surefire way to kill any amusement they might have derived from the situation.

Know Yourself, Love Yourself

Self-awareness is a lifelong pursuit. But with your busy schedule, you might not be in tune with your own body. For example, did you know that the average person farts ten to twenty times per day, amounting to around 500 to 1,500 milliliters of gas daily? Most of it is produced by gut bacteria. Ever wonder why beans cause flatulence? They (and some other legumes, vegetables, fruits, and grains) contain complex carbohydrates, which the body can't digest on its own. These carbohydrates pass through the stomach and small intestine and into the large intestine, where most gut bacteria reside, and where the bacteria eat and ferment the carbohydrates and expel gas. (That said, some gas is from swallowed air.)

Foods containing sulfur make the bacteria produce smelly, sulfurous gases. But these farts are only about 1 percent of flatulence. Most farts are caused by hydrogen, carbon dioxide, and methane. They occur without us even acknowledging them, silent and odorless. But they are happening. And they mark the passing of minutes, hours, days, and seasons.

MEASURE A DAY IN THE GAS YOU PASS

Spend the next day recording as many farts as you can, and two or three words describing how you felt at the moment they were released.

Fart #   **Fart Feeling**

_____   I felt_____

_____   I felt_____

_____   I felt_____

_____   I felt_____

_____   I felt_____

Making an Offering to the Porcelain God

There are many reasons you might vomit: too much alcohol, contaminated food, ingested toxins, morning sickness, stomach virus, motion sickness, migraine, pain, overeating, or even emotional distress. Some diseases and disorders can also cause vomiting. Maybe you've thrown up when you haven't eaten in hours and wondered where all the yellowish liquid came from. The answer: your small intestine. The complex process of vomiting includes the step of relaxing the pyloric sphincter between the stomach and small intestine and squeezing the contents back into the stomach before expulsion.

Sometimes puke is inevitable, and you usually shouldn't stop it because it is a way your body expels toxins. But if it's due to nerves or motion sickness, you can eat saltines or ginger, or take nausea medication. Also, there is a pressure point called P6 on your inner forearm, the width of three fingers from your wrist, which soothes the stomach. If stress is the problem, relaxation techniques may also help. But if the vomiting persists or any other alarming symptoms are present, see a doctor ASAP.

BOWING TO THE PORCELAIN GOD

Finish doodling this altar to That Which Accepts All Crap.

What's in a Name?

Mastication: that's the proper word for chewing.

There are lots of proper, fancy names for the processes of the digestive system, but we rarely use them. We know what defecation and urination are, but we tend to refer to them by slang terms, such as poop or pee.

A bolus is a mass of your already chewed food. Deglutition is the fancy word for swallowing your food and drink. Eructation is burping, and a burp is a ructus. The ancient Roman term for excessive burping was ructabundus. You might guess the meaning of flatus, which is the buildup of gas in the gut, which leads to flatulence. And we've already covered borborygmus (gut growling).

Regurgitation is a longer word for vomiting, but even the experts tend to stick with vomiting. Sometimes simple is best.

HOW WELL DID YOU READ THAT?

Don't cheat. Match the term and its meaning.

Mastication	excessive burping
Bolus	buildup of gas
Deglutition	chewing
Ructabundus	swallowing
Flatus	chewed food

Gut Feelings

Your wondrous brain allows you to do many things. But you have another brain, the gut brain (the enteric nervous system, or ENS), which you must appease daily.

The ENS has the same neuroreceptors as the brain in your head. Gut-to-brain communication takes place via the vagus nerve, but the ENS can control digestive functions even if its link to the central nervous system is severed, possibly because the digestive system evolved before the brain did.

Some 95 percent of the feel-good neurotransmitter serotonin is produced in the gut, where it stimulates muscle movement and regulates the immune system. It gets released into the bloodstream and makes it to the actual brain, where it influences emotion.

It is hypothesized that gut bacteria may affect cravings by producing amino acids, which pass into the bloodstream and travel to the brain. There they get converted to dopamine and serotonin. Researchers also now believe that gastrointestinal distress can cause mood disorders. So do what it takes to appease your gut. A happy gut means a happy you.

FEELING ALL THE FEELS

Aside from the living crap in your gut, what is currently bringing you happiness?

_____

_____

_____

_____

_____

_____

_____

_____

_____

Put Your Gut to the Test

Symptoms of Parkinson's disease often manifest first in the digestive system. When scientists do an intestinal biopsy of these patients and examine the gut neurons, they see the same sort of lesions found in brain neurons of patients diagnosed with Parkinson's, giving hope that someday a liver biopsy—a less risky procedure than a brain biopsy—can be a test for this disease.

Recent research at Caltech found a potential link between the gut biome and Parkinson's disease, meaning the illness might actually start in the gut. Mice were genetically modified to produce too many alpha-synuclein fibers, which clump and damage neurons in Parkinson's patients. Mice raised in a nonsterile environment developed the motor symptoms of the disease, but mice raised in a sterile environment had fewer symptoms.

Antibiotics (which can wipe out gut flora) improved the condition of the symptomatic mice. When the low-symptom mice were injected with gut bacteria from humans, some with Parkinson's and some without Parkinson's, the ones injected with the Parkinson's patients' bacteria developed motor difficulties.

GRATITUDE FOR THAT GUT FLORA

Color in this representation of all the helpful little creatures that are at this very moment living inside you.

CHAPTER 6

Asanas--Poses and Practices That Move Things Along

Can Sound Make You Poop?

There has long been talk of a "brown noise," which can make people poop their pants involuntarily, and rumors have circulated about this very thing having happened at various musical events.

But scientists, including researchers at NASA, and the *MythBusters*, poo-poo the existence of the sound. So far, no experiments have produced the desired (or undesired) result. One thing that may have fueled rumors of the note was the testing of the Republic XF-84H prototype supersonic jet, aka the "Thunderscreech," in 1956. Its propellers produced shock waves that reportedly caused seizures, nausea, and bowel disruptions. The plane was understandably not put into production, but despite rumors to the contrary, the noise itself wasn't to blame.

Another was a 1974 *New Scientist* parody article that claimed a giant horn demonstrated at the Great Exhibition of 1851 in London caused mass diarrhea, but it was, alas, a joke. So you can go to your next air show or concert without fear of a stray note causing an embarrassing accident.

A PLAYLIST TO DEUCE BY

Craft your own calming pooping playlist: Make a behindfulness playlist to accompany your bathroom "meditations."

1. _____

_____

2. _____

_____

3. _____

_____

4. _____

_____

5. _____

_____

Coffee Run

Savor that morning cup of coffee, but not too far from the bathroom. Along with the life-prolonging benefits of its antioxidants and the energy boost from its caffeine, coffee may also get your intestines moving. In 30 to 40 percent of people, drinking coffee (regular or decaf) quickly triggers peristalsis, making them need to go number two in just a few minutes. Scientists are unsure what causes this effect. One hypothesis is that your morning cup of joe contains chlorogenic acid, which both adds to the acid already in your stomach and causes the stomach to create more gastric acid. The effect decreases over time for regular drinkers.

Make your coffee drinking and pooping experience more meta with kopi luwak, the coffee made from beans that are fermented in the digestive tract of a civet cat, pooped out, and processed into an expensive delicacy of a drink.

Have that morning brew to wake up both your brain and your bowels, and start them on their day's journey.

WHAT ELSE IS GETTING YOU MOVING?

Reflect on the passions, goals, and upcoming events in your life that help you get up in the morning, stay regular, and keep moving.

Walk It Out

If you have trouble with constipation, one easy remedy is going for a walk. The longer food takes to move through your system, the more water your body removes from it, making your stool dryer and harder, leading to constipation. Exercise in general helps push the food along at a faster pace. Aerobic exercise, such as walking, running, cycling, dancing, or swimming, seems particularly good at moving things along.

The exact physiological reasons have yet to be pinpointed, but some theories are that exercise stimulates the release of hormones that affect the intestines, that it increases neural activity in the gut, and that it makes blood flow away from the GI tract, causing it to contract.

Wait an hour or so after eating to exercise. You don't want to send blood away from your gastrointestinal system when it's hard at work digesting your food, as this can slow down the passage of food. Keeping that caveat in mind, the next time your BMs are difficult, walk it out.

A WALK FOR REGULARITY

What are your five all-time favorite walks, strolls, or hikes?
Make a promise to follow one of these paths again soon.

1. _____

   _____

2. _____

   _____

3. _____

   _____

4. _____

   _____

5. _____

   _____

Yoga Can Help You Poop

Yoga dates from around 3500 BCE in India and involves specific stretches and poses (asanas), breath control practices (pranayama), and meditation techniques to help bring the mind and body into harmony. Practicing yoga can improve your flexibility, help you relax, and improve your mood and sense of well-being in general.

And it can also apparently help you poop. A 2015 study found that yoga could ease some of the symptoms of irritable bowel syndrome, including constipation, gas, and abdominal pain. Many of the recommendations involve poses that twist and stretch the abdominal area, along with other poses for the rest of the body, and breathing and meditation exercises. There's even a pose referred to as Pavanamuktasana (the "wind-relieving pose"). So feel free to let go of gas and excrement without shame for the sake of your physical and mental comfort. But maybe save the latter for after yoga class.

TWIST TO YOUR LOO

Try this simple chair yoga pose to keep things moving correctly.

Take Strain Out of Your Life

When stool collects in your rectum, it is kept in place by the puborectalis, a muscle that surrounds your rectum. When contracted, this muscle keeps your colon bent so you don't lose control of your bowels. When you sit on a Western toilet, there is still a slight bend in your colon. But when you squat, this muscle relaxes and the colon is straighter, requiring less straining. People in Africa and Asia, where squatting toilets are common, have less constipation and fewer hemorrhoids (the latter can be caused by straining).

Use a Squatty Potty or similar device to change your posture on the john. The Squatty Potty is a little stool you put your feet on, which raises your knees to mimic a squat. Studies show that such a device leads to emptying the bowels more quickly and completely, as well as less straining. Use a stool to help that other type of stool move along, and take the strain out of your bathroom life.

TRY POOPING RIGHT FOR ONCE

Here's a meditative pose to help things move. If you don't already have a Squatty Potty, put your feet up on a stool (no, not that type of stool). With a straight back, lean forward and rest your elbows on your knees. Close your eyes, be in the moment, and let your bowels do their thing.

Exercise Your Sphincter

Embrace aging! Except for the preventable parts. Pelvic floor muscles weaken as we age, which can lead to leaks of urine, stool, or gas. Kegels (pelvic floor exercises) can help both men and women retain control of their bladders and bowels and prevent pelvic organ prolapse in women.

Gynecologist Arnold H. Kegel developed these exercises in the 1940s. Squeeze the pelvic floor muscles, holding for a few seconds, and relaxing for a few seconds, around ten times in one session, and alternate with ten quick flexes lasting 1 second. Aim for thirty or forty Kegels a day, starting with 3- to 5-second squeezes and building up to 10 or more seconds.

To find the right muscles, pretend you are avoiding farting. Men can also start to pee and then stop it, and women can squeeze as though tightening around a tampon. Do them on your own or seek help from a medical professional.

You can do Kegels just about anywhere—even at work. Don't do them regularly while actually peeing, though, as this can lead to a urinary tract infection.

A LITTLE EXERCISE

Okay, let's try a minute of Kegel exercises to work that pelvic floor. What could be better? (Remember: To find the right muscles, pretend you are avoiding farting. Men can also start to pee and then stop the stream, and women can squeeze as though they are tightening around a tampon.)

On your mark. Go.

SQUEEZE
HOLD
AND
RELAX

Where the Sun Now Shines

There's a hot new trend: perineum sunning. Influencers say it's a way to increase energy and gain the same vitamin D benefits as being in the sun for hours. But it may just leave you smarting in a sensitive place.

The perineum is the tissue between genitals and anus. Perineum sunning involves exposing your perineum to direct sunlight for a few minutes by lying naked (at least from the waist down) on your back and pulling your ankles toward your head to expose this area to that fiery disk in the sky.

The sun-deprived nature of this area makes it more susceptible to sunburn, which could lead to skin cancer down the road. UV light can also cause herpes flare-ups and increase the risk of cancer for people with HPV-induced warts. Most dermatologists recommend applying sunscreen (or clothing) to any part of your skin that might get exposed to sunlight. There is also no science to support the health claims. So maybe keep it in your pants, and take some vitamin D.

THE SUNLIGHT CURE

What else could use a little time out in the open? What are some things you've been carrying around quietly that are stressing you out? Spread some light on them.

_____

_____

_____

_____

_____

_____

_____

_____

To Bidet, or Not to Bidet

In the United States, Joseph Gayetty first marketed his "medicated" water closet paper in 1857. The rest is history.

But there may be a better way—the bidet. This device sprays your backside with a stream of water, and most bidets can be set to different angles. They come as stand-alone units, but you can also buy dual-purpose toilets with built-in bidet features, fancy bidet seats, relatively cheap attachments, and handheld manual devices.

If you want to save trees, you might want to switch. As for the health benefits, the jury is out. One study showed that using a bidet reduced anorectal pressure, which bolsters reports that they help with hemorrhoids and anal fissures. There are also claims that they help prevent urinary tract infections and constipation. But there are no in-depth studies that prove these claims.

Aside from the ecological benefits, people report that their posteriors feel cleaner than with wiping. So there is no harm in trying out a bidet for that freshly cleansed feeling.

BAD HABITS

Over the years, we accumulate habits that are just not necessary. Some waste time (and even paper) that you could use to lead a more fulfilling life. List old habits that you'd like to eliminate. And in their place, list new ones to try. Cleanse your life of wasteful traditions.

_____

_____

_____

_____

_____

_____

_____

_____

That Fart Stench Could Save Your Life

This practice teaches us that being present in the here and now can be therapeutic—connecting the mind to the behind. Research from the University of Exeter provides us with a deeper understanding of this relationship. According to the research, the hydrogen sulfide gas that makes our flatulence stink can be targeted at the mitochondria within our cells to protect them, keeping cells alive that might otherwise die.

Mitochondria (tiny structures within each cell) have their own DNA, generate energy to keep the cell going, and work to control inflammation—a condition linked to a host of ill health effects. Cells in distress already take in enzymes to produce hydrogen sulfide to protect their mitochondria and keep themselves alive. Researchers developed a compound called AP39, which can target tiny amounts of hydrogen sulfide directly at mitochondria, taking advantage of this protective effect. This therapy could potentially be used to reduce the risk of a range of issues, including high blood pressure, obesity, diabetes, arthritis, heart attack, dementia, and stroke.

STOP AND SMELL THE HYDROGEN SULFIDE

Although the smell of your own "silent giant" may be familiar to you, how often do you really stop and admire the subtle nuances of each wafting fart? Indeed, what you ate recently, the time of day, the ambient temperature, and even the fabric of your pants can change the way you experience the gift of gas.

Take the time to record the nose feel of your farts:

❏ eggy

❏ floral

❏ cheese

❏ freshly cut cabbage

❏ nosy ale

❏ expired broccoli

❏ gym shoes

❏ old man's sweater

❏ stormy seas

Let It All Out

Enemas, aka colon cleanses or colonic irrigation, are often touted as a way to flush the toxins out of the body, providing all sorts of health benefits. But there is doubt as to whether they do any good, and they can do a great deal of harm if done badly. Enemas involve placing a tube in the rectum and pumping in water and other substances, including coffee. They can cause minor side effects, such as nausea, diarrhea, or bloating. But they can also result in more serious harm, such as rectal tearing, dehydration, damage to gut flora, infection, or an imbalance in electrolytes. Coffee enemas have been linked to several deaths due to the latter two side effects.

With proper nutrition, hydration, and health, we flush out our own toxins. So eat well, hydrate, and let your colon flush itself. Trust your body to detoxify on its own.

UNLOAD AND FORGIVE

Detoxify your soul by forgiving all those who have harmed you. Make a list and jettison all thoughts of your past maltreatment. (But detoxify your colon by simply eating, hydrating, and going to the bathroom as usual.)

_____

_____

_____

_____

_____

_____

_____

_____

CHAPTER 7

Reaching Enlightenment

Waste of Space

The space age heralded wonderful advancements, but space plumbing lagged behind. Alan B. Shepard, the first American in space, was also the first to wet his spacesuit. His *Mercury* launch was delayed for hours after he was suited up and strapped in. He advised mission control that he had to pee, and they told him to urinate in his spacesuit. NASA had urinary collection worked into subsequent suits.

Gemini and *Apollo* missions were equipped with urine and fecal bags. Because gravity is an important factor in waste excretion, but nonexistent en route to the moon, the fecal bags had a finger pouch used to manually guide the poop into the bag. After pooping, the astronaut had to add a germicide and massage it in to keep fecal bacteria from generating gas—so that the bag didn't explode! There were mishaps. Transcripts from the *Apollo 10* mission include the astronauts noticing, dealing with, and joking about the appearance of a couple of floating turds in the cabin. That is truly a situation where it is difficult to remain calm.

WHEN THE GOING GETS TOUGH

Contemplate the difficult journey of life ahead of you. List five things that you aspire to achieve on your path to enlightenment, and five tough climbs that are going to help you get there.

1. _____

2. _____

3. _____

4. _____

5. _____

1. _____

2. _____

3. _____

4. _____

5. _____

Go with the Flow

Sometimes you have to go with the flow and let the current carry you—and sometimes it's an air current. NASA developed a toilet for the space shuttle with airflow to pull things along so that a finger wasn't necessary. But the toilet was not without problems. The early one had a spinning blade that blended the feces and the toilet paper, after which the combination was freeze-dried by the extreme cold of space. Bits of freeze-dried muck would float into the cabin. That was fixed, but excrement still doesn't behave in zero gravity. Another zero-G phenomenon, dubbed fecal popcorning, involved poop bouncing against the walls and sometimes flying back toward the astronaut. If an astronaut didn't shut the sliding door before the poop reached the exit, it could freeze dry and jam the slider shut or escape into the spacecraft.

NASA is launching a new portable Universal Waste Management System for testing on the International Space Station. It's compact, accommodates female anatomy, and treats urine before it goes into the station's recycling system for water extraction.

LET'S TRY THAT AGAIN

Nobody likes to fail. Especially when that means you have literal shit floating around your house. But it's no reason to stop trying! What are some things you've failed at that deserve a second moon shot?

_____

_____

_____

_____

_____

_____

_____

_____

_____

_____

Eat Shit and Live

If someone told you to eat shit, you'd be insulted. But, it could be a blessing. We are learning more about the importance of the microbiome, and the bad things that can happen if you deplete your own. But how do you get it back, or get healthy flora if you've never had it before? Now it is possible to more thoroughly repopulate the gut with healthy bacteria—from a healthy donor.

Sometimes after a person has lost some gut biome, bacteria called Clostridium difficile fill the gap. This pathogen causes gut inflammation and diarrhea. But a new therapy, fecal bacteriotherapy (fecal transplantation), is 90 percent effective. It involves administering another person's feces nasally or rectally.

Tom Gravel, one brave, industrious man with Crohn's disease, decided to try it for himself. He had a healthy neighbor whom he convinced to give him a supply of feces. Using techniques he had read about, he ingested the fecal material over a couple of years and reversed his symptoms. But don't try this at home. You are just as likely to introduce a new pathogen into your system.

BORROW A LITTLE JOY

Think of your favorite people and animals in your life. What things that bring them joy can you transplant into your own life?

_____

_____

_____

_____

_____

_____

_____

_____

_____

Nurture the Arid Wasteland

Some areas in the world have no ready supply of water, and in some places indoor plumbing is scarce. According to the World Health Organization, around 2.3 billion people lack access to toilets. As in the ancient world, when clean, safe toilets are absent, disease occurs.

The dry toilet, sometimes called a composting toilet (although the compost may not be safe to use in gardens), is one possible solution. There are different types. Some involve depositing both liquid and solid waste in the same container and throwing sawdust on top. Others separate liquid and solid waste, which allows solid waste to break down more quickly. (Urine turns into ammonia. When it is present, it kills the bacteria that break down feces.) And others use insects, such as soldier fly larvae or earthworms, to eat and reduce the waste. Dry toilets require more maintenance than traditional water toilets, and the waste must be removed and taken away at some point. But some don't have to be emptied for years. And they are a definite improvement on the outhouse.

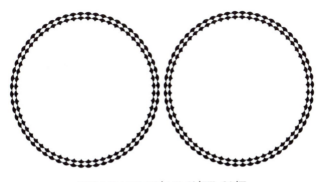

SEPARATE THAT SHIT OUT

Write your favorite characteristics of yourself in the bubbles at the top, and note the things you'd like to change down below. Focus on what makes you feel great about yourself! And work to improve the frustrations about yourself you want to transform.

The Power of Pee and Poop

Urine- and feces-powered fuel cells already exist. Researchers have developed microbial fuel cells that incorporate bacteria and feed on wastewater. The bacteria within a cell oxidize (combine with oxygen) organic compounds in the waste, which releases electrons that power the cell.

The University of California, Irvine, and FuelCell Energy Inc. developed a fuel cell that breaks hydrogen off of methane molecules. It is used at a California waste treatment plant to create fuel to power the plant, and excess fuel is sold. Toyota is using the cells to produce hydrogen fuel from methane generated by cow dung at a plant in California.

Even fatbergs (see page 54) are being converted to biofuel at a plant that first filters out the gunk through esterification, which chemically changes the fat, and then distills the result and mixes it with regular diesel.

BioCycle in South Africa feeds soldier flies on sewage sludge, presses them to extract oil, and sells the oil as fuel. We are in a great new age of waste power.

ENERGIZE YOUR LIFE

Let's get moving! Write down 5 things you want to get done this month. Then do them!

1. _____

_____

2. _____

_____

3. _____

_____

4. _____

_____

5. _____

_____

Let Go of Shame

Expressing yourself can be good for the soul. But in many cultures, including our own, expressions of bathroom-related subjects, especially pooping, are taboo. We don't talk about our bowel movements, or the color and consistency of our pee and poop, or any difficulties we might have in that arena, even though they could hold some clues to our health.

At best we let people know when we are going to the restroom (a word that doesn't quite capture the nature of our activities there), or ask if we can use their bathroom. This dynamic is pretty odd since peeing and pooping are things we have to do nearly every single day for our entire lives.

But there is one group hoping to change this reticence to speak the truth: the POOP Project. It stands for the People's Own Organic Power, and the group works to foster conversations about sanitation so that we can let go of the guilt associated with a necessary bodily function, and so that we can address the sanitation needs of the world head-on. They've even spoken before the UN.

BALANCE YOUR SHAME WITH LOVE

Write down all the things in life that secretly get you down.
Say them out loud! And then balance out each of those
elements with things that bring you pride and joy.

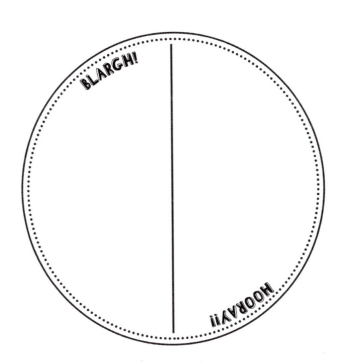

BLARGH!

HOORAY!!

References

Ailes, Emma. "Scotland and the indoor toilet." *BBC News*. April 19, 2013. https://www.bbc.com/news/uk-scotland-22214728.

Albee, Sarah. *Poop Happened!* New York: Bloomsbury, 2010.

Alice, Matthew. "Sterculius, the Roman god of feces." *San Diego Reader*. February 3, 1994. https://www.sandiegoreader.com/news/1994/feb/03/straight-sterculius-god-feces.

"Animals & Plants - Dung Beetle." San Diego Zoo. Accessed January 10, 2021. https://animals.sandiegozoo.org/animals/dung-beetle.

Anthony, Sebastian. "The Fuel Cell That Turns Poop into Power." *ExtremeTech*. August 20, 2012. https://www.extremetech.com/extreme/134741-the-fuel-cell-that-turns-poop-into-power.

"Are You Pooing Properly?" Queensland Health. Last modified October 22, 2019. https://www.health.qld.gov.au/news-events/news/how-to-poo-properly-sit-squat-healthy.

"At-Home Thyroid Testing Kits: What We Know... and What We Don't. An Interview with Dr. Hyesoo Lowe." Columbia Thyroid Center. Accessed January 25, 2021. https://columbiasurgery.org/news/home-thyroid-testing-kits-what-we-knowand-what-we-dont.

Bailey, Regina. "Salivary Amylase and Other Enzymes in Saliva." ThoughtCo. Last modified February 26, 2019. https://www.thoughtco.com/salivary-amylase-other-enzymes-in-saliva-4586549

Bass, Gary. "The Athenian Plague, a Cautionary Tale of Democracy's Fragility." *The New Yorker*. June 10, 2020. https://www.newyorker.com /culture/culture-desk/the-athenian-plague-a-cautionary-tale -of-democracys-fragility.

Beck, Julie. "Roman Plumbing Overrated." *The Atlantic*. January 8, 2016. https://www.theatlantic.com/health/archive/2016/01/ancient-roman -toilets-gross/423072.

Blumer, R.H. *Wiped: The Curious History of Toilet Paper.* New York: Middlemarch Media Press, 2013. Kindle edition.

"The Brain-Gut Connection." Johns Hopkins Medicine. Accessed on January 21, 2021. https://www.hopkinsmedicine.org/health/wellness -and-prevention/the-brain-gut-connection.

"A Brief History of the Flush Toilet." The British Association of Urological Surgeons. Accessed January 17, 2021. https://www.baus.org.uk /museum/164/a_brief_history_of_the_flush_toilet.

"Bus-Sized Fatberg Weighing 40 Tonnes Cleared from London Sewer." *The Guardian*. October 29, 2019. https://www.theguardian.com /environment/2019/oct/29/bus-sized-fatberg-cleared-from -london-sewer.

Bushak, Lecia. "A Brief History of Bathing; The Importance of Hygiene, from Ancient Rome's Sophisticated Showers to the Modern Day." *Medical Daily*. December 11, 2015. https://www.medicaldaily.com /brief-history-bathing-importance-hygiene-ancient-romes -sophisticated-showers-modern-364826.

Coghlan, Andy. "Natural-Born Painkiller Found in Human Saliva." *NewScientist*. November 13, 2006. https://www.newscientist.com /article/dn10514-natural-born-painkiller-found-in-human-saliva.

Cummings, Jack. "I Went in Search of the 'Brown Note', the Frequency That Makes You Shit Yourself." *Vice.* November 24, 2016. https://www.vice.com/en_us/article/ppv35z/in-search-of-the-brown-noise.

Cunha, Burke A. "The Cause of the Plague of Athens: Plague, Typhoid, Typhus, Smallpox, or Measles?" *Infectious Disease Clinics of North America* 18, no. 1: 29–43. March 2004. https://www.ncbi.nlm.nih.gov/pmc/articles/PMC7118959.

Denjean, Cecile, dir. *The Gut: Our Second Brain.* 2014; France: MagellanTV.

"The Development of the Flushing Toilet." Twyford Bathrooms. Accessed January 18, 2021. https://www.twyfordbathrooms.com/-/media/twyfordnew/en/about-us/history/thedevelopmentoftheflushingtoilet.ashx?la=en&hash=EB32B31549223F2574FC278DF4DAA907757F4D57.

Dialynas, E.G. and A.N. Angelakis. "The Evolution of Water Supply Technologies in Ancient Crete, Greece." World Water Museum. Accessed July 13, 2020. http://docplayer.net/34228208-The-evolution-of-water-supply-technologies-in-ancient-crete-greece-e-g-dialynas-1-and-a-n-angelakis-2.html.

Domanico, Anthony. "Smelling Farts Could Be the Best Thing You Do Today." C/NET. July 11, 2014. https://www.cnet.com/news/how-smelling-farts-could-save-your-life.

Dove, Laurie. L. "How Can Straining on the Toilet Kill You?" *HowStuffWorks.* Accessed January 25, 2020. https://health.howstuffworks.com/human-body/systems/digestive/can-straining-on-toilet-kill.htm.

Elshaikh, Eman M. "Ancient India—Indus River Valley Civilizations." Khan Academy. Accessed July 13, 2020. https://www.khanacademy.org

/humanities/world-history/world-history-beginnings/ancient-india/a
/the-indus-river-valley-civilization.

Enders, Giulia. *Gut*. Read by Katy Sobey. Newark: Greystone Books,
2016.

Evans, Lisa. "6 Scents That Can Transform Your Mood and Productivity."
Entrepreneur. October 8, 2012. https://www.entrepreneur.com
/article/224575

"Exercise to Ease Constipation." *WebMD*. Last modified June 17, 2020.
https://www.webmd.com/digestive-disorders/exercise-curing
-constipation-via-movement.

Feltman, Rachel. "Here's Why Coffee Makes You Poop." *The Washington
Post*. August 10, 2015. https://www.washingtonpost.com/news
/speaking-of-science/wp/2015/08/10/why-does-coffee-make-you
-poop.

Fletcher, Jenna. "8 Yoga Poses to Relieve Constipation." *Medical News
Today*. November 21, 2019. https://www.medicalnewstoday.com
/articles/327086.

"Forgotten and Underrated Goddesses —Cloacina, Goddess of the
Sewers." MookyChick. December 1, 2017. https://www.mookychick
.co.uk/health/witchcraft-spirituality/forgotten-underrated-goddesses
-cloacina-goddess-sewers.php.

Friml, Irwin. "The Collophone Commemorated." *New Scientist*.
December 26, 1974. https://books.google.co.uk/books?id=khzDRYfj97
AC&pg=PA932&lpg=PA932&dq=the+collophone+commemorated
&source=bl&ots=vrgUH_MUh4&sig=Z2nnGZJ6W3_Ph_gzXKuh
XCbLfWo&hl=en&sa=X&ved=0ahUKEwie2pKZw7_QAhWsJcAK
HdllCYEQ6AElGzAA#v=onepage&q&f=false.

George, Rose. *The Big Necessity: The Unmentionable World of Human Waste and Why It Matters*. New York: Metropolitan Books, 2008.

Gill, Dr. Fiona. 2013. "Coprolite Chemistry - what fossilised faeces can tell us about extinct animals." Filmed July 6, 2012 in London, England. Royal Society video, 28:30. https://youtu.be/vQL8elYXurl.

Gilman, Sylvie and Thierry de Lestrade, dirs. *Microbiota: The Amazing Powers of the Gut*. 2019; France: MagellanTV.

Goulson, Dave. "The Beguiling History of Bees." *Scientific American*. April 25, 2014. https://www.scientificamerican.com/article/the-beguiling-history-of-bees-excerpt.

Gray, Richard. "'Fatbergs', Faeces and Other Waste We Flush Could Be a Fuel." *BBC*. October 5, 2017. https://www.bbc.com/future/article/20171005-human-waste-could-be-the-fuel-of-the-future.

Groth, Leah. "So, Perineum Sunning Is a Thing Now—Here's Why Doctors Definitely Don't Want You to Try It." *Health Magazine*. February 21, 2020. https://www.health.com/mind-body/perineum-butt-sunning-wellness-trend.

Guilford, Gwynn. "The Hogs That Created America's First Urban Working Class." *Quartz*. July 16, 2017. https://qz.com/1025640/hogs.

Handwerk, Brian. "Feeling Overtaxed? The Romans Would Tax Your Urine." *National Geographic*. April 14, 2016. https://www.nationalgeographic.com/news/2016/04/160414-history-bad-taxes-tax-day/.

Handwerk, Brian. "It's Not Just Bears: These Hibernating Animals May Surprise You." National Geographic. March 7, 2019. https://www.nationalgeographic.com/animals/2019/03/animals-winter-hibernation-turtles/.

Hsieh, Carina. "Does Sunning Your Asshole Actually Have Any Health Bennies?" *Cosmopolitan*. December 10, 2019. https://www.cosmopolitan.com/sex-love/a30183958/perineum-sunning-benefits.

Hoffman, Matthew, MD. "Picture of the Esophagus." WebMD. Last modified July 10, 2020. https://www.webmd.com/digestive-disorders/picture-of-the-esophagus.

Hoffman, Matthew, MD. "Picture of the Intestines." WebMD. Last modified May 18, 2019. https://www.webmd.com/digestive-disorders/picture-of-the-intestines.

Hoffman, Matthew, MD. "Picture of the Stomach." WebMD. Last modified July 10, 2020. https://www.webmd.com/digestive-disorders/picture-of-the-stomach.

"How Does the Tongue Work?" Institute for Quality and Efficiency in Health Care. Last modified August 23, 2016. https://www.ncbi.nlm.nih.gov/books/NBK279407/#_NBK279407_pubdet.

"How to Get More Probiotics." Harvard Medical School. Last modified August 24, 2020. https://www.health.harvard.edu/staying-healthy/how-to-get-more-probiotics.

"How to Make Pomander Balls." Old Farmer's Almanac. https://www.almanac.com/content/how-make-pomander-balls.

"How Your Septic System Works." EPA. https://www.epa.gov/septic/how-your-septic-system-works.

"Indus Civilization." *Encyclopaedia Britannica*. Last modified March 3, 2020. https://www.britannica.com/topic/Indus-civilization.

Johnson, David L., PhD, Kenneth R. Mead, PhD, Robert A. Lynch, PhD, and Deborah V.L. Hirst, PhD. (2013) "Lifting the Lid on Toilet Plume Aerosol: A Literature Review with Suggestions for Future Research."

American Journal of Infection Control 41, no.3: 254-258. March 2103. https://www.ncbi.nlm.nih.gov/pmc/articles/PMC4692156.

Jones, Paul Anthony. "The Proper Names of 17 Bodily Functions." *Mental Floss.* July 23, 2017. https://www.mentalfloss.com/article/61450/proper-names-17-bodily-functions.

"Joseph Bazalgette (1819-1891)." BBC. Accessed January 18, 2021. http://www.bbc.co.uk/history/historic_figures/bazalgette_joseph.shtml.

Kavuri, Vijaya, Nagarathna Raghuram, Ariel Malamud, and Senthamil R. Selvan. "Irritable Bowel Syndrome: Yoga as Remedial Therapy." Evidence-Based *Complementary and Alternative Medicine.* May 6, 2015. https://www.ncbi.nlm.nih.gov/pmc/articles/PMC4438173.

"Kegel Exercises." WebMD. Last modified July 21, 2020. https://www.webmd.com/women/guide/kegels-should-i-do-them.

Keim, Brandon. "Life's Complexity Began with Poop." *Wired.* December 5, 2007. https://www.wired.com/2007/12/lifes-complexit.

Kelly, Kevin. "Set Your Bowel Disruptor to Explosive Diarrhea." *Gizmodo.* February 20, 2008. https://io9.gizmodo.com/set-your-bowel-disruptor-to-explosive-diarrhea-358446.

Killgrove, Kristina. "6 Practical Ways Romans Used Human Urine and Feces in Daily Life." *Mental Floss.* March 14, 2016. https://www.mentalfloss.com/article/76994/6-practical-ways-romans-used-human-urine-and-feces-daily-life.

Koloski-Ostrow, Ann Olga. "What Toilets and Sewers Tell Us about Ancient Roman Sanitation." Phys.org. November 19, 2015. https://phys.org/news/2015-11-toilets-sewers-ancient-roman-sanitation.html.

Kumar, Mohi. "From Gunpowder to Teeth Whitener: The Science Behind Historic Uses of Urine." *Smithsonian Magazine.* August 20, 2013.

https://www.smithsonianmag.com/science-nature/from-gunpowder
-to-teeth-whitener-the-science-behind-historic-uses-of-urine-442390.

Kwong, Waldan K., Luis A. Medina, Hauke Koch, Kong-Wah Sing,
Eunice Jia Yu Soh, John S. Ascher, Rodolfo Jaffé, and Nancy A. Moran.
"Dynamic Microbiome Evolution in Social Bees." *Science Advances*.
March 29, 2017: Vol. 3, no. 3, e1600513. https://advances.sciencemag
.org/content/3/3/e1600513.full.

"Lactose Intolerance." Mayo Clinic. April 7, 2020. https://www
.mayoclinic.org/diseases-conditions/lactose-intolerance/symptoms
-causes/syc-20374232.

"Latest Hands-Free Electronic Water Faucets Found to Be Hindrance,
Not Help, in Hospital Infection Control." Johns Hopkins Medicine.
March 31, 2011. https://www.hopkinsmedicine.org/news/media
/releases/latest_hands_free_electronic_water_faucets_found
_to_be_hindrance_not_help_in_hospital_infection_control.

Le Trionnaire, Sophie, etc. 2014. "The Synthesis and Functional
Evaluation of a Mitochondria-Targeted Hydrogen Sulfide Donor,
(10-oxo-10-(4-(3-thioxo-3H-1,2-dithiol-5-yl)- phenoxy)decyl)
triphenylphosphonium bromide (AP39)." *Medicinal Chemistry
Communication* 5 (April): 728-736. https://www.researchgate.net
/profile/Sophie_Le_Trionnaire/publication/262842178_The_synthesis
_and_functional_evaluation_of_a_mitochondria-targeted_hydrogen
_sulfide_donor_10-oxo-10-4-3-thioxo-3H-12-dithiol-5-ylphenoxydecyltrip
henylphosphonium_bromide_AP39/links/02e7e539019396b6b0000000
/The-synthesis-and-functional-evaluation-of-a-mitochondria-targeted
-hydrogen-sulfide-donor-10-oxo-10-4-3-thioxo-3H-1-2-dithiol-5-ylphenox
ydecyltriphenylphosphonium-bromide-AP39.pdf?origin=publication
_detail.

Lindbergh, Ben. "Social Distancing Diaries: Cut the Crap and Embrace the Bidet." The Ringer. March 23, 2020. https://www.theringer.com /coronavirus/2020/3/23/21190414/social-distancing-diaries-bidet -toilet-paper-shortage.

Little, Becky. "It Took Surprisingly Long for Doctors to Figure Out the Benefits of Hand Washing." History Channel. March 6, 2020. https:// www.history.com/news/hand-washing-disease-infection.

Marineli, Filio, Gregory Tsoucalas, Marianna Karamanou, and George Androutsos. 2013. "Mary Mallon (1869-1938) and the History of Typhoid Fever." *Annals of Gastroenterology* 26, no. 2: 132-134. https://www.ncbi .nlm.nih.gov/pmc/articles/PMC3959940.

Martin, Rebecca. "Minoan Water Harvesting and Distribution (Terracotta Pipes)." *The Civil Engineer*. Accessed January 13, 2021. https:// www.thecivilengineer.org/online-historical-database-of-civil -infrastructure/item/383-minoan-water-harvesting-and-distribution -terracotta-pipes.

Mazzotta, Marta, Luna Girolamini, Maria Rosaria Pascale, Jessica Lizzadro, Silvano Salaris, Ada Dormi, and Sandra Cristino. "The Role of Sensor-Activated Faucets in Surgical Handwashing Environment as a Reservoir of Legionella." *Pathogens*. June 5, 2020: vol. 9, no. 6: 446. https://www.ncbi.nlm.nih.gov/pmc/articles/PMC7350366.

Miller, Korin. "Why Does Drinking Coffee Always Make You Poop?" *Health Magazine*. July 30, 2019. https://www.health.com/condition /digestive-health/why-does-coffee-make-you-poop.

"The Mission." The POOP Project. Accessed January 14, 2021. https:// thepoopproject.org/mission.

Nall, Rachel. "Would I Benefit from a Coffee Enema?" Medical News Today. February 7, 2017. https://www.medicalnewstoday.com /articles/315663.

Nash, Stephen E. "What Did Ancient Romans Do Without Toilet Paper?" *Sapiens*. April 3, 2018. https://www.sapiens.org/column /curiosities/ancient-roman-bathrooms.

Nathanson, Jerry A. and Archis Ambulkar. "Wastewater Treatment." *Encyclopaedia Britannica*. October 29, 2020. https://www.britannica .com/technology/wastewater-treatment.

"Nausea and Vomiting." WebMD. Last modified December 6, 2020. https://www.webmd.com/digestive-disorders/digestive-diseases -nausea-vomiting.

"New Evidence Suggests Parkinson's Might Not Start in the Brain." The Cure Parkinson's Trust. December 5, 2016. https://www.parkinson.org /blog/science-news/science-article/evidence-parkinsons-begins-in-gut.

NIDDK. "Your Digestive System and How it Works." NIH. December 2017. https://www.niddk.nih.gov/health-information/digestive -diseases/digestive-system-how-it-works.

Oberhaus, Daniel. "Why NASA Designed a New $23 Million Space Toilet." *Wired*. June 22, 2020. https://www.wired.com/story /why-nasa-designed-a-new-dollar23-million-space-toilet.

Ohnsman, Alan. "Green Fuel from a Brown Source." *Edmonton Journal*. June 7, 2008. https://www.pressreader.com/canada/edmonton-jour nal/20080607/282518654249885.

Ohnsman, Alan. "Toyota to Turn Cow Manure into Hydrogen to Back Its Fuel Cell Vehicle Push." *Forbes*. November 30, 2017. https://www.forbes .com/sites/alanohnsman/2017/11/30/toyota-to-turn-cow-manure -into-hydrogen-to-back-its-fuel-cell-vehicle-push.

Oliwenstein, Lori. "Life's Grand Explosions." *Discover Magazine*. January 1, 1996. https://www.discovermagazine.com/planet-earth/lifes-grand-explosions.

"Our Story." Royal Doulton. Accessed January 18, 2021. https://www.royaldoulton.com/en-us/discover/our-story.

"Paltrow-Promoted Coffee Enema May Be Dangerous." WebMD. January 10, 2018. https://www.webmd.com/women/news/20180108/paltrow-promoted-coffee-enema-may-be-dangerous.

Palus, Shannon. "Are Bidets Better for You Than Toilet Paper?" *New York Times*. September 7, 2016. https://www.nytimes.com/wirecutter/blog/bidets-better-than-toilet-paper.

Picco, Michael F., MD. "Is Colon Cleansing a Good Way to Eliminate Toxins from Your Body?" Mayo Clinic. June 3, 2020. https://www.mayoclinic.org/healthy-lifestyle/consumer-health/expert-answers/colon-cleansing/faq-20058435.

"Picture of the Appendix." WebMD. Last modified May 18, 2019. https://www.webmd.com/digestive-disorders/picture-of-the-appendix.

Ponti, Crystal. "All the Ways We've Wiped: The History of Toilet Paper and What Came Before." History. April 15, 2020. https://www.history.com/news/toilet-paper-hygiene-ancient-rome-china.

"The Poo Theory of Life." *Environmental News Network*. November 30, 2007. https://www.enn.com/articles/26207-the-poo-theory-of-life.

Poynter, Elizabeth. *Bedbugs and Chamberpots: A History of Human Hygiene*. 2016. Elizabeth Poynter.

Ramanujan, Krishna. "Study Challenges Widely Held Assumption of Bee Evolution." *Cornell Chronicle*. November 15, 2018. https://news.cornell.edu/stories/2018/11/study-challenges-widely-held-assumption-bee-evolution.

Roach, Mary. *Packing for Mars*. New York: W.W. Norton & Company, 2010.

Rogers, Nala. "Inside the Controversial World of Composting Toilets." *Inside Science*. June 14, 2019. https://news.cornell.edu/stories/2018/11 /study-challenges-widely-held-assumption-bee-evolution.

"Roman Aqueducts." *National Geographic*. Last modified July 6, 2018. http://www.nationalgeographic.org/encyclopedia/roman-aqueducts.

"Rotten Egg Gas Holds Key to Healthcare Therapies." University of Exeter. July 9, 2014. http://www.exeter.ac.uk/news/research/title _393168_en.html.

"Saliva." *Encyclopaedia Britannica*. Last modified November 3, 2017. https://www.britannica.com/science/saliva.

"Saliva and Your Mouth." WebMD. Last modified October 10, 2019. https://www.webmd.com/oral-health/what-is-saliva.

Saunders, Chas, and Peter J. Allen, eds. "Cloacine: Goddess of the Sewers." Godchecker. Last modified September 9, 2018. https://www .godchecker.com/roman-mythology/CLOACINA.

Saunders, Chas, and Peter J. Allen, eds. "STERCULIUS: To Put It Politely, He Is the God of Poop." Godchecker. Last modified September 9, 2018. https://www.godchecker.com/roman-mythology/STERCULIUS.

Schlinger, Amy. "Why Do I Have to Poop When I Exercise?" *The Healthy*. August 13, 2020. https://www.thehealthy.com/digestive-health /why-exercise-makes-you-poop.

Shiel, William C., Jr MD. "Medical Definition of Cloaca." *MedicineNet*. Accessed July 18, 2021. https://www.medicinenet.com/cloaca /definition.htm.

"Signs and Symptoms of Acute Hepatic Porphyria." WebMD. Last modified January 20, 2021. https://www.webmd.com/brain/acute-hepatic-porphyria-symptoms.

Slotkin, Jason. "Behold the Fatberg: London's 130-Ton, 'Rock-Solid' Sewer Blockage." NPR. September 12, 2017. https://www.npr.org/sections/thetwo-way/2017/09/12/550465000/behold-the-fatberg-london-s-130-ton-rock-solid-sewer-blockage.

Stamp, Jimmy. "From Turrets to Toilets: A Partial History of the Throne Room." *Smithsonian Magazine*. June 20, 2014. https://www.smithsonianmag.com/history/turrets-toilets-partial-history-throne-room-180951788.

"Step-by-Step Guide to Performing Kegel Exercises." Harvard Medical School. Last updated September 16, 2019. https://www.health.harvard.edu/bladder-and-bowel/step-by-step-guide-to-performing-kegel-exercises.

Stromberg, Joseph. "Everybody Farts. But Here are 9 Surprising Facts about Flatulence You May Not Know." *Vox*. August 11, 2015. https://www.vox.com/2014/12/4/7332411/fart-flatulence.

"The Structure and Function of the Digestive System." Cleveland Clinic. Last modified September 13, 2018. https://my.clevelandclinic.org/health/articles/7041-the-structure-and-function-of-the-digestive-system.

"Surprising Ways Alcohol May Be Good for You." WebMD. Last modified September 3, 2020. https://www.webmd.com/diet/ss/slideshow-alcohol-health-benefits.

Tiwari, Manjul. 2011. "Science Behind Human Saliva." *Journal of Natural Science, Biology, and Medicine* 2, No. 1 (Jan.–June): 53-58. https://www.ncbi.nlm.nih.gov/pmc/articles/PMC3312700/#__ffn_sectitle.

"Tongue." *Encyclopaedia Britannica*. Last modified August 1, 2019. https://www.britannica.com/science/tongue/additional-info#history.

"Urine Color." Mayo Clinic. October 24, 2020. https://www.mayoclinic.org/diseases-conditions/urine-color/symptoms-causes/syc-20367333.

Walters, Jennipher. "5 Probiotic Foods with Good Bacteria for Your Gut." *Shape*. April 21, 2011. https://www.shape.com/healthy-eating/diet-tips/5-good-you-foods-healthy-bacteria-your-stomach.

"What is a Squatty Potty?" WebMD. Last modified October 8, 2019. https://www.webmd.com/digestive-disorders/squatty-potty-what-is.

"What Kind of Poop Do I Have?" WebMD. Last modified January 16, 2020. https://www.webmd.com/digestive-disorders/poop-chart-bristol-stool-scale.

Wills, Amanda. "The First American in Space Wore a Pee-Soaked Spacesuit." *Mashable*. May 5, 2014. https://mashable.com/2014/05/05/alan-shepard-pee-spacesuit.

About the Author

Dr. Harry B. Hind is the leading expert on behindfulness in the United States. Having earned his doctorate in Zen Bootyism at the University of Santa Cruz, Dr. Hind has helped millions of people reimagine the role of their rear ends. His behindfulness workshops and award-winning Toilet Talks have been featured in countless news, entertainment, and medical outlets.